Cornelia Haas · Ulrich Renz

My Most Beautiful Dream

Il mio più bel sogno

Bilingual children's picture book

with online audio and video

Translation:

Sefâ Jesse Konuk Agnew (English)

Clara Galeati (Italian)

Audiobook and video:

www.sefa-bilingual.com/bonus

Password for free access:

English: **BDEN1423**

Italian: **BDIT1829**

Lulu can't fall asleep. Everyone else is dreaming already – the shark, the elephant, the little mouse, the dragon, the kangaroo, the knight, the monkey, the pilot. And the lion cub. Even the bear has trouble keeping his eyes open ...

Hey bear, will you take me along into your dream?

Lulù non riesce ad addormentarsi. Tutti gli altri stanno già sognando – lo squalo, l'elefante, il topolino, il drago, il canguro, il cavaliere, la scimmia, il pilota. E il leoncino. Anche all'orso stanno crollando gli occhi ...

Ehi orso, mi porti con te nel tuo sogno?

And with that, Lulu finds herself in bear dreamland. The bear catches fish in Lake Tagayumi. And Lulu wonders, who could be living up there in the trees?

When the dream is over, Lulu wants to go on another adventure. Come along, let's visit the shark! What could he be dreaming?

E così Lulù è già nel paese dei sogni degli orsi. L'orso cattura pesci nel lago
Tagayumi. E Lulù si chiede chi potrebbe mai vivere là su quegli alberi?
Quando il sogno è finito, Lulù vuole provare qualcos'altro. Vieni, andiamo
a trovare lo squalo! Che cosa starà sognando?

The shark plays tag with the fish. Finally he's got some friends! Nobody's afraid of his sharp teeth.

When the dream is over, Lulu wants to go on another adventure. Come along, let's visit the elephant! What could he be dreaming?

Lo squalo sta giocando ad acchiapparella con i pesci. Finalmente ha degli amici! Nessuno ha paura dei suoi denti aguzzi.

Quando il sogno è finito, Lulù vuole provare qualcos'altro. Venite, andiamo a trovare l'elefante! Che cosa starà sognando?

The elephant is as light as a feather and can fly! He's about to land on the celestial meadow.

When the dream is over, Lulu wants to go on another adventure. Come along, let's visit the little mouse! What could she be dreaming?

L'elefante è leggero come una piuma e può volare! Sta per atterrare sul prato celeste.

Quando il sogno è finito, Lulù vuole provare qualcos'altro. Venite, andiamo a trovare il topolino! Che cosa starà sognando?

The little mouse watches the fair. She likes the roller coaster best.
When the dream is over, Lulu wants to go on another adventure. Come
along, let's visit the dragon! What could she be dreaming?

Il topolino sta guardando la fiera. Gli piacciono particolarmente le montagne russe.

Quando il sogno è finito, Lulù vuole provare qualcos'altro. Venite, andiamo a trovare il drago! Che cosa starà sognando?

The dragon is thirsty from spitting fire. She'd like to drink up the whole lemonade lake.

When the dream is over, Lulu wants to go on another adventure. Come along, let's visit the kangaroo! What could she be dreaming?

Il drago, a furia di sputare fuoco, ha sete. Gli piacerebbe bersi l'intero lago
di limonata.

Quando il sogno è finito, Lulù vuole provare qualcos'altro. Venite, andiamo
a trovare il canguro! Che cosa starà sognando?

The kangaroo jumps around the candy factory and fills her pouch. Even more of the blue sweets! And more lollipops! And chocolate!
When the dream is over, Lulu wants to go on another adventure. Come along, let's visit the knight! What could he be dreaming?

Il canguro sta saltando nella fabbrica di dolciumi e si riempe il marsupio.

Ancora caramelle blu! E ancora lecca-lecca! E cioccolata!

Quando il sogno è finito, Lulù vuole provare qualcos'altro. Venite, andiamo a trovare il cavaliere! Che cosa starà sognando?

The knight is having a cake fight with his dream princess. Oops! The whipped cream cake has gone the wrong way!

When the dream is over, Lulu wants to go on another adventure. Come along, let's visit the monkey! What could he be dreaming?

Il cavaliere sta facendo una battaglia di torte con la principessa dei suoi sogni. Oh! La torta alla panna va nella direzione sbagliata!
Quando il sogno è finito, Lulù vuole provare qualcos'altro. Venite, andiamo a trovare la scimmia! Che cosa starà sognando?

Snow has finally fallen in Monkeyland. The whole barrel of monkeys is beside itself and getting up to monkey business.

When the dream is over, Lulu wants to go on another adventure. Come along, let's visit the pilot! In which dream could he have landed?

Finalmente ha nevicato in Scimmialandia! L'intera combriccola di scimmie non sta più nella pelle e si comportano tutte come in una gabbia di matti. Quando il sogno è finito, Lulù vuole provare qualcos'altro. Venite, andiamo a trovare il pilota! In che sogno potrebbe essere atterrato?

The pilot flies on and on. To the ends of the earth, and even farther, right on up to the stars. No other pilot has ever managed that.

When the dream is over, everybody is very tired and doesn't feel like going on many adventures anymore. But they'd still like to visit the lion cub.

What could she be dreaming?

Il pilota vola e vola ancora. Fino ai confini della terra e ancora più lontano, fino alle stelle. Non ce l'ha fatta nessun altro pilota.

Quando il sogno è finito, sono già tutti molto stanchi e non vogliono più continuare a provare così tanto. Però il leoncino, vogliono ancora andare a trovarlo. Che cosa starà sognando?

The lion cub is homesick and wants to go back to the warm, cozy bed.
And so do the others.

And thus begins ...

Il leoncino ha nostalgia di casa e vuole tornare nel caldo, accogliente letto.
E gli altri pure.

E là inizia ...

... Lulu's
most beautiful dream.

... il più bel sogno
di Lulù.

The authors

Cornelia Haas has been illustrating childrens' and adolescents' books since 2001. She was born near Augsburg, Germany, in 1972. She studied design at the Münster University of Applied Sciences and is currently a professor on the faculty of Münster University of Applied Sciences teaching illustration.

Ulrich Renz was born in Stuttgart, Germany, in 1960. After studying French literature in Paris he graduated from medical school in Lübeck and worked as head of a scientific publishing company. He is now a writer of non-fiction books as well as children's fiction books.

Do you like drawing?

Here are the pictures from the story to color in:

www.sefa-bilingual.com/coloring

Sleep Tight, Little Wolf

For ages 2 and up

with online audio and video

Tim can't fall asleep. His little wolf is missing! Perhaps he forgot him outside?
Tim heads out all alone into the night – and unexpectedly encounters some friends ...

Available in your languages?

► Check out with our „Language Wizard":

www.sefa-bilingual.com/languages

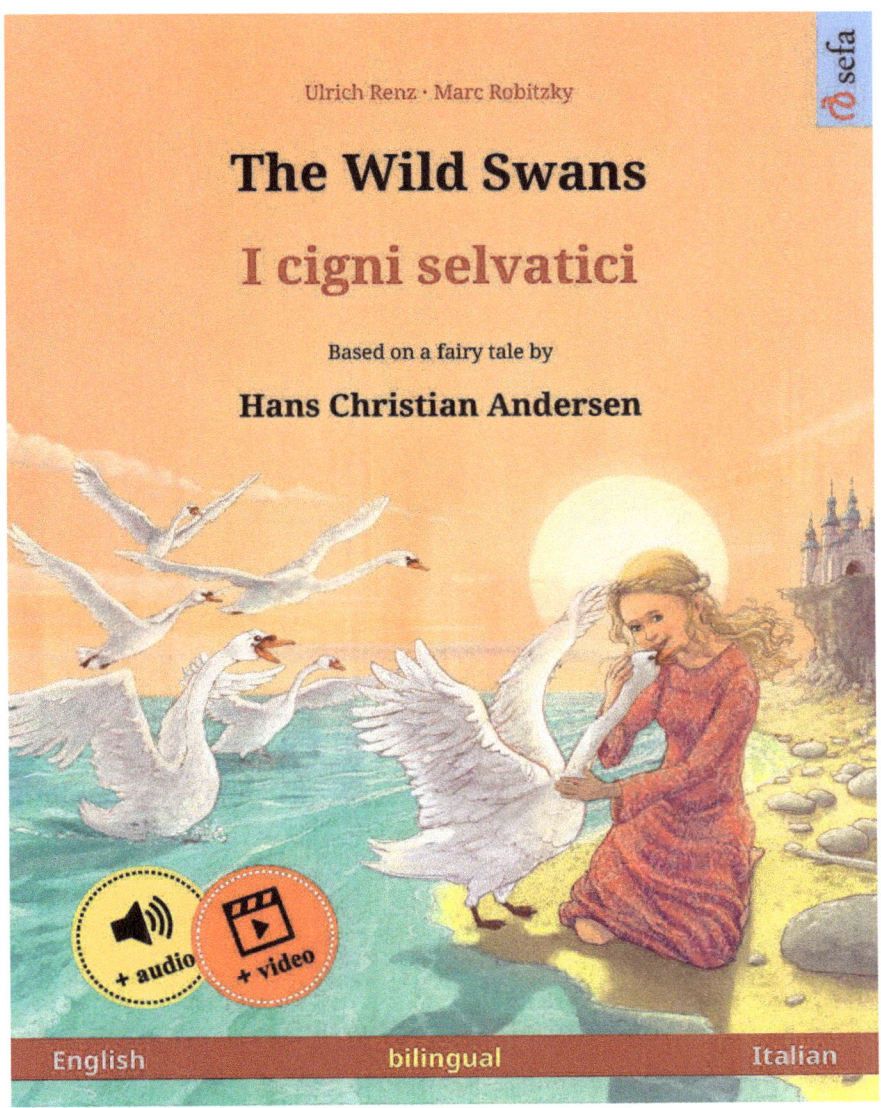

Ulrich Renz · Marc Robitzky

The Wild Swans
I cigni selvatici

Based on a fairy tale by

Hans Christian Andersen

+ audio   + video

English   bilingual   Italian

The Wild Swans

Based on a fairy tale by
Hans Christian Andersen

Recommended age: 4-5
and up

„The Wild Swans" by Hans Christian Andersen is, with good reason, one of the world's most popular fairy tales. In its timeless form it addresses the issues out of which human dramas are made: fear, bravery, love, betrayal, separation and reunion.

Available in your languages?

► Check out with our „Language Wizard":

www.sefa-bilingual.com/languages

© 2024 by Sefa Verlag Kirsten Bödeker, Lübeck, Germany
www.sefa-verlag.de

Special thanks to Paul Bödeker, Freiburg, Germany
Font: Noto Sans

ISBN: 9783739963785